TRAUMA'S DEATH

Deanna Repose Oaks

TRAUMA'S DEATH

First paperback edition September 2022

Book design by Deanna Repose Oaks

ISBN-13: 978-1-956482-03-4 (paperback)

Published by View from Room 217, LLC
www.viewfromroom217.com

To Karen
The idea started writing itself as I dropped my armor down
Because I needed to witness the ripples as it hit the ground
This book is now my beacon, growing brighter with every thought
As emotions inside were swirled and caught

To Natalie
You set goals for me to reach
A new book every year
This is the second time I failed you
But know it is ALMOST here

To Jessica
Thanks for the bat, both literally & figuratively!

FOREWARD

An argument triggered emotions so big that I found myself
curled up on the floor in a ball, crying with heaving sobs.
That same argument also stopped me in my tracks.
Trauma's Death was the poem I wrote just after the end of
that argument, as a way of me solidifying what I must do to
beat my demons once and for all. When I read it (because I
wrote it in a blind emotional state) I forced myself through
the new perspective I discovered, a perspective that
changed my entire outlook on life. The poem was evidence
of that shift. As the shift widened, changed, and grew into a
life of its own, the other poems in this collection were just
THERE. I can't explain it, and I don't really want to. I want
you to feel what you feel without me jumping in and saying
what you should feel or that you are wrong for feeling that
way – because you aren't wrong. Your feelings are yours,
mine are mine. Emotions are never wrong; it is the
perception of how we handle the *expressing* of our
emotions that make others tell us our emotions are wrong.
The emotions never are.

As I write this forward, 32 days after the being urged to
write this book, there are 30 poems in the collection, and 25
of them are brand spanking new. I have never written
anything this quickly, and never with this much excitement
to share.

And while I know it isn't "right" to celebrate death with
gusto, I'm celebrating this one with all my heart.

TABLE OF CONTENTS

Trauma's Death

I am too busy keeping my trauma to see his
Too busy to know what's then, what's tomorrow, what is
I refuse to see the care he puts in, afraid it will disappear
All the while pushing him away trying to make real my fear
Easier to blame him than me
But only when I'm causing what's come to be
Easier to disassociate than assimilate
And then blame everything on fate
I need to stop holding onto trauma
Keep myself from causing drama
Put myself in others' shoes
See the world in realistic hues
And while you feel the argument was wasted breath
This is growth towards trauma's death

My Mirror

The mirror I look into every day
Warped now beyond recognition
Changes a little every morning
By the thoughts of who I think I am
A little more with every look
Until it could hang in a carnival fun house
Concave face and stretched limbs
Bulging middle and clown feet
Everything but reality
There is no way to see the stunning light
Or the smile hiding within
Or the joy I have to give
Or the lives I enhance by being
All I see is a carnival oddity
Not able to be normal
Separate from all

Where's my baseball bat?

Note To Self

The evil words you said...
Still echo through my head
They reverberate off my skull
With a pain, steady and dull
Until they are used again

Once repeated, the echoes' pain
Take on a solid, horrifying refrain
They tag along with every new compliment
Telling me I am not fit
Even when they aren't said again

How do I take the power from these words?
How do I keep them forever unheard?
Who knows who is going to say what, when?
Because the fear of hearing them again...

I need to replace the echoes with something else
Something I believe, truly, from within myself

I just have to find it

Note to self:
Do not look in:
- the bottom of the bottles
- or at the ends of the needles
- or through the lines on the mirrors;

You got lost on that path once before, and it is now so
much clearer...

Where you will find the real you → is in your heart, beating true

My Voice

"I don't want to hear your voice"
Is it really THAT bad?

"Yes."

So, I mumble unintelligible sounds
Too quiet to be heard
Hoping you can't unwant to hear
What you can't hear me say

In the forced silence, I write
Hoping my words SCREAM from the page

Without the thoughts you invoked
Or the silence I was made to fill
Without the struggle you put me through
There wouldn't be such strong emotions to distill
I'm grateful you didn't want to hear

MY VOICE

For I wouldn't be where I am today
Sharing my silent screams
Overcoming all of my yesterdays
Living out all my dreams

Knowing I have something you can't touch
If you had only felt how much

I truly loved

Climbing Out of Chinese Hell

A paper cut, so shallow, no one can tell
Hurts like hell
No treatment needed (no blood oozes)
Except, maybe, through drugs & boozes
Another one, ouch, a bit deeper
Pain lasts longer, must be a keeper

Slices too many to count

A ream of paper shred
Hurt constant in my head
The art of cutting, honed
Still 500 more left to go

My skin so tender, can't stand touch
It all just aches so very much
Still, no blood, even with cuts
Deep as bone

Can't stand the gaping, non-bleeding wounds
I grab for the last page from the stack...

WAIT! I need to fight past this urge
So my pain inside can surge
Out past what was horrible then
Back to myself, way back when
I was happy, true, and bright
Before we met that horrid night

Once I beat my urges, I will finally be able to say

"The Chinese have a lot of hells, Jack"
Used to be our favorite movie misquote, a long way back

Recirculating Hearts

We are, EVEN THOUGH our skins are different shades
We are, EVEN THOUGH our shapes are different sizes
We are, EVEN THOUGH our brains think different thoughts
We are, EVEN THOUGH our love shows in different ways

While we cannot control our EVEN THOUGHs...
We can control the way our blood flows

Through our hearts

We can choose to color our hearts black as night
Forcing blood to bleed outright
We can choose to color our hearts a deep, deep red
Forcing blood to bleed from others instead
We can choose to color our hearts with brilliance
Rainbows
Puzzle Pieces
Unicorns
Forcing blood to recirculate acceptance

How Do We Choose?

There are a million paths before us
> Some worn down to dirt
> Some covered in rose petals
> Some made of upright shards of glass

How do you choose the one to take?
> The one everyone else takes?
> The prettiest one?
> The one that will make you bleed with every step?

Not knowing what is at the end...
> Sameness?
> A cliff that falls into a never-ending abyss?
> A new you?

Or knowing what is here and now...
> Acceptance?
> Love?
> Pain?

What if you never get to the end...
Being strong isn't walking the path others have taken before you
Being strong isn't walking the path made soft by others
Being strong is taking the painful step,
> learning how to take the next one so that it won't be
> even with the knowledge you may never get to the end
> learning to walk FOR YOU & adapting to pain, is strength

Sting of Rejection

The bee stings deep, then dies
The wasp stings deeper, then flies
The love stings deepest, then rejects
Every single, wonderful aspect

My mother, the bee
My daughter, the wasp
My exes, the love
They taught me rejection, beyond and above

But healing only begins
Once forgiveness wins

I forgive

Telephone Game

The six of us sit in a circle and our play goes like this:
I whisper to my trauma 1
My trauma 1 whispers to his trauma 1
His trauma 1 whispers to him
He whispers to his trauma 2
His trauma 2 whispers to my trauma 2
My trauma 2 whispers to me

He says "I love you."	I hear "I'll leave you."
I say "I'll be right back."	He hears "I'll never be back."
He says "Did you take out the trash?"	I hear "She never does what I ask."
I say "Did you do the dishes?"	He hears "You failed at doing your job."

As the rounds continue, more players join in...
>Anger and resentment.
>Blame and regret.
>Joy and love.
>Happiness and dreamfulness.
>Indifference and pain.

Neither one of us, him or me, remembered the most
important rule of the game:
Compare the statement said with the statement heard.
We just kept going round and round in circles, adding more
players with each round.
Until all we heard were our own failures.
>Time to start following the rules.

Perspective

How do you define perspective?

Is it the angle from which you view a painting
Or the angle the artist painted?
Is it the character you identify with
Or the narrator of the story?
Is it the instrument you hear the most
Or the words of the song?
Is it the view from where you stand in a room
Or the side of the argument you are on?

Once defined, can it change?

Changing perspective isn't about wearing someone else's
     shoes
Or even seeing things from a different point of view
It is changing how you INTERACT with the thoughts
     being thunk
Removing yourself from the problem and all that junk.

Music, Movies, TV, Books

Books show me worlds unknown
Give me advice, outside my own
TV gives me formats clear
The hero always wins here.
Movies have glitter, plot, and glamor
Please more twists and turns I clamor

Music is the thing that cleanses my soul
Changes my heartbeat, makes me whole
Beats and words and emotions true
Rhymes in lyrics, better than violets blue
Dancing in the kitchen, singing with a brush*
Losing myself in a rush
Letting go, breathing in
All the feelings within

*See My "Pick Me Up" Playlist for the most played in my kitchen

Tin Cans

Tin cans attached to the car
Just Married seems like such fun
But you drag your problems with you
No matter how far you run

The cans bounce harder
As the terrain gets treacherous
They cause most damage
When you slack to confess

The cans make noise
Bounce off the road
Held by unbreakable chains
No matter if driven or towed

The Hike

Once plopped at the bottom of a canyon
Climbing out appears impossible
Stuck between too sheer walls
With a river flowing through the bottom too rough to raft
Plenty of water when in need of drink
Plenty of food if you know how to fish

You have three choices:
Toil to claw yourself to the top
Allow yourself to flow with the water
Stay where you are

Each choice has its perils and highs
Each choice has its certainty and lows
Each choice holds regrets of the other two

Art of Love

With every love a painting was created
Then hung proudly in a gallery
Before long they were ready for a show
When critics arrived
The first one's reviews were less than stellar
Curling the paint
But still, the masses came in droves
Before long, the paintings were ruined
They couldn't keep their hands to themselves
Vandalized beyond recognition
Paint thrown directly from 5 gallon paint cans
Knives ran through the canvases
The spoiled art left hanging in broken frames
For all to see

Then, one day, the gallery was closed to the public
The paintings removed from the walls
The canvasses removed from their broken frames
Rolled up in a tight sleeve
Put away, out of sight
Where they will stay until needed again
There's no need to loathe them every day

Fixed the frames up real nice
Canvassed them in bright white and solid black
Doing my best from looking back
And painting on my own

Circling The Drain

Stuck in a whirlpool
Circling the drain
Navigating the waters
Trying in vain
Using a shipwreck
That's already seen
The bottom of the ocean
And everything between

The shipwreck needs sails
And a warm wind to blow
To stay out of the abyss
Of the drain down below
The deepness inches closer
As the water slips in
The wreck no match
Gravity will win

The rudders can be set
At just the right angle
To use the whirlpool
And exit the tangle

The water still falls
Down into the drain
Even when the wreck
Is within its sea lane

Keep the lighthouse in sight
Whenever you sail
So the drain won't consume
And your ship won't derail
The light will guide you
To a safe harbor to dock
And maybe, just maybe
You'll land at Plymouth Rock

Self-Evident

We hold these truths to be self-evident, that all men are created equal, that they are endowed by their Creator with certain unalienable Rights, that among these are Life, Liberty and the pursuit of Happiness.

- Declaration of Independence, July 4, 1776.

Self-evident to who? Or is it whom? Or is it they?
I'm so confused I don't know what to say
Self-evident has never been true to me
Because my Self is twisted, full of debris
There is nothing Evident about my life
Even if the skin I have is white
Because I am woman, I can roar
But I still hit the ceiling when I try to soar
Then there's the Portuguese surname and Mexican brood
And the Irish eyes with attitude
It's hard to pursue happiness in all of this mess
Because I am always declared something less
But I am more and those rights belong to me too
For people like me, remember, we are Americans true

I Am ~~Special~~ ~~Different~~ Same

When I was four
My mom said I was special
Because I didn't come from her tummy
But from an unknown mommy somewhere else
Being special made me extra different
Standing next to twins no one could tell apart
Not blood of my blood and all of that
Differences pointed out
Used against me
Time and again
No DNA traits, failed biology
Can't be sisters
Nothing alike
But we are, even after our differences,
FAMILY
We can be the same
If we choose

I chose

Organizing Labels

We label everything
People, places, things
Few of them accurate
Yet we still apply them
To everything we see
Perhaps for purpose
Organize them in our thought
Those people, places, and things
The labels, personal
May not mean the same to the labeled
Offensive in nature
For their very existence
As they limit the person, place, or thing
To the definition of the label
Leave everything unlabeled
Causes chaos of thought

Stop Saying What Everyone Says

"Get over it" that's what she advised
As if it is as easy as opening the blinds
Sometimes it's too hard to even open my eyes

"Get Over it" that's what he said
As if it is as easy as getting out of bed
Sometimes it's too hard to even get out of my head

I worked and I worked to try and fix it
Only to slide backwards

"Get over it" that's what they screamed
As if it was easy to make it less than it seemed
Sometimes it is so very hard to be redeemed

I swear if I hear "Get over it" one more time...

My brain does not work like yours
You need to allow me growth
And failure
Just Stop.

My Cocoon

It started with buying blackout curtains so I could sleep
Then closing the blinds to keep people from peeping
Then wrapping myself in hoodies and blankets to keep
    warm within the darkness
Everything layered just so... so no one could see

ME

The layers captured and held the darkness close
My normal became ripe territory for disease and mold
The wrappings constricted over time
Tightening to the point of suffocation
As I struggled for life against the restraints
I found my wings
Full of color, ready to fly, still wrapped inside
But I knew they too would succumb
To the disease and mold of the darkness
If I didn't let in some light
But I held the wrappings too long too tightly
My fear expanded, causing panic and pain
As the struggle continued
My desire to see the colors full on my wings
Drove me on, through the agony and hysteria
Until a pinprick of light bled through

The light in you

My Horde

I take the blame
For things that go wrong
When they are out of my control

I take the blame (and pile it on)
Especially when you yell
When it is beyond my control

I sit with my blame day and night
Shaping it into my faults
Always believing every wrong is mine
I hold them close

My collection is of faults for things that aren't mine

Ring Around the Rosie

They were standing in a ring
In the center of the street
Circled around, sharing a secret

Ring around the crack pipe
Pockets full of rocks
Flame to glass
We all fall down

Around the ring went the pipe
Smashed to the ground
I just saved my life

Looking the Part

With a passion for acting yearning to burn
I showed up smiling, happy, ready to learn
I walked into the classroom, full of sass
Looking the part, for one of them, I'd pass
The "it" girl drinking free at fancy bars
Spoiled rotten by daddy, driving fancy cars
Just a 22-year-old living the dream
At least to them, that was what they seen
Until my ex-boyfriend showed up wielding a knife
Did I reveal I was running for my life
They were shocked when I let them know
I also had a two-year-old in tow
They saw me, this pretty, thin, young girl
They didn't see the tragedies life likes to hurl
It started before I was born
A clothes hanger, a womb, a uterus torn
Then came the family, all sorts of wrong
I didn't fit in or get along
Then there was the guy who pinned me on the couch
He had his way, did his thing, ouch
Then the shrink who told me to run away
I'd be better off hooking than if I stay
Then the life flushed down the drain
Leaving me such a long-lasting pain
Then the car, the only roof over my head
Then the addict who was nice and shared his bed
Then the baby we both adore
Then the iron through the door
Then the drunk who let me down

26

When his friend came back to town
Those were just things that happened during my days
Somehow, they became a passing phase
Every morning I got up and faced the day new
Because of everything else I got through
I didn't look back, because I didn't want to see
I just overcame to be the smiling me
I thought I'd learn to pretend in acting class
But the only thing I learned was I already had.

Projections

There is a screen between you and me
It holds echoes of your thoughts
And reflects your feelings
Over the shadows of my actions

So while my actions are mine
The thoughts haven't crossed my mind
Nor have the feelings crossed my heart

But while I feel the screen
I cannot push it aside
For it follows my actions

Explaining the screen has proven nothing
And without the proof
There is no belief

Your words of "You would feel the same way, I know you"
Mean nothing to me
Because I see the screen
I hear the echoes of your thoughts
I feel the reflections of your feelings

But all you see is who you think I am

Blow Torches and Missiles

Opening the bathroom door into a fire
As the can of hair spray emptied in flame
Running down the hall, falling to the floor
Dodging the empty bottle's thrown aim
Seeing the bottle still embedded into the wall
From last week's launch
Reminds me to avoid the bathroom
And my most evil hater
Still to this day, I barely brush my hair
Or try to be pretty in any way
I still hear the whoosh as I enter

My Love

I learned a long time ago
That my love is mine to give
You can't take it from me
You can't give it to me
All you can do is show me yours
As I show you mine
I can show you mine
Even when you don't show me yours
I can see your love hidden underneath
And will try to draw it to the surface
But I will not force anything
I will not make you be someone you don't want to be
Just show you how far you can go
When you let your love show.

My Gift

It was wrapped so beautifully under the tree
Silver paper, red ribbon, bow
I saw my name in pretty script
I was waiting for the right day

Next thing I knew, days passed
The silver paper, red ribbon, bow
Held a new name in less pretty script
But still there all the same

My name now in block print
Across a trashed brown bag
I didn't think anything less
Both were gifts

I just wanted the one meant for me

Being Poetic

I am excited to share
I am scared
Are these poems poetic?
Too much of me? Not enough?
Will you see you in them?
Poetic as a literary sense is just a poem
Poetic as a poetic sense is a crying jag
While I strive for emotional poeticness
I feel I just end up with poems
Yet I keep writing
Because after each poem
My emotions are gone
Trapped on the page

Sunshine

The sun rises over fluctuating gas prices,
Wreaking havoc on the safety of glass devices,
Casting shadows when met with bone and skin,
Alluding to the greatness we have within.
With the world so dark, I crave the day
When the sun truly chases darkness away.
Until then, I sneak from my bland brown desk
Each and every chance I get.

I play in the sunshine, all day and night,
Basking in all of the glorious light
Searing yellow rays chase away lows;
While silver light hues create calm shadows.
Such contrast, this reflection's glare,
From the magnifying power of a Windows® square.

When your heart sinks instead of sails,
The solar panel cracks, the power line fails,
Know the brightest star in the daytime sky
Has so much power it lights the night.
To harness this power and give it to you
My greatest hope wishes to...

Lift your spirits toward the sky,
So you can see this power fly
Through the clouds, above the rain,
Showing you you will rise again.

Rainbows

Sometimes you need to
CREATE a storm
To see the

at

THE END

My "Pick Me Up" Playlist

Just the Way You Are - Billy Joel
F**kin' Perfect - P!nk
Invincible - Pat Benetar
Beautiful - Christina Aguilera
Confident - Demi Lovato
Titanium - Madilyn Bailey's Cover
Can't Blame a Girl for Trying - Sabrina Carpenter
This is Me - The Greatest Showman cast recording*
A Million Dreams - P!nk
Little Do You Know - Alex & Sierra
Happy - Pharrell
Try - Callie Colbert
This is Why We Can't Have Nice Things - Taylor Swift
Get Back Up Again - Anna Kendrick
Better Place - Rachel Platten
Human - Christina Perri
I Will Always Love You - Whitney Houston's cover
Cups - Anna Kendrick
Fight Song - Rachel Platten
Firework - Katy Perry
Silent Lucidity - Queensryche
Turn the Page - Metallica's cover
Drawing Flies - Soundgarden
Drive - Incubus
The Unforgiven – Metallica
Wake Up – Julie and the Phantoms cast Season 1
Shake It Off - Taylor Swift
The Star-Spangled Banner* - Whitney Houston's cover
Blaze of Glory - Bon Jovi

*These songs make me cry EVERY time I hear them
List referenced by the poem: Music, Movies, TV, Books

Made in the USA
Columbia, SC
07 October 2022